ARCADES TAROT

HAIKU POEMS

CAMELIA ELIAS

ARCADES TAROT
HAIKU POEMS

EYECORNER PRESS

© Camelia Elias | 2019

All rights reserved.

Arcades Tarot: Haiku poems

Published by EyeCorner Press

in the series **Divination Books**

August 2019, Thy, Denmark

ISBN: 978-87-92633-45-3

Cover design, image and layout: Camelia Elias

Images of the Tarot: *Arcades Tarot* by Camelia Elias

Arcades Tarot (2019) is a limited edition Art Tarot, built around the unique Carolus Zoya Tarot (ca.1760) in the author's private collection and copyright.

*Secret affinities:
palm tree and feather duster,
hair dryer and Venus.*

– *WALTER BENJAMIN*
The Arcades Project

CONTENTS

Prologue 9

Haiku poems 13

Epilogue 71

PROLOGUE

One card for one haiku has been seen before. Six cards for one haiku, not so much. This book of poems explores the challenge of fitting the essence of six Tarot cards together into the constricted syllabic pattern of the haiku: 5, 7, 5. Magic numbers.

Initially the book had another function than the poetic. It accompanied the Arcades Tarot, an art tarot limited to 22 copies, designed with this question in mind: Why do all the cards always face one direction, left or right? Placed in a mirror, a different perception arises. I wanted to explore it.

I took out the unique and ancient Carolus Zoya Tarot in my collection, and staged it. I placed the trump cards in front of a wooden mirror. Talismanic objects were also selected. My own hair orchestrated the puppetry. The light came through it, and strange shadows appeared. Several planes came together through the arcades. I noticed that my perception didn't change much after seeing the cards in their mirror image. This was to be expected, given that we can only perceive things because we have a language to articulate what we see. Here the name of the cards in the mirror appeared the most strange.

If something else changed, it was the sense of temporality as culturally convened upon. Visually, when we look to the left, we think that the past is there. When we look to the right, we say that the future is there. This is all nonsense, of course. Yet much of the standard approach to reading the Tarot cards relies on such conventions, with readers often saying things like this: 'In the past you were depressed, but things are improving,' if, for instance, the cards on the table would be the Moon, the Hermit, and Judgment. In the mirror, the Hermit looks to the right, so we get a different sense of urgency here. No more contemplations of the past. Now it's all a forward movement. And yet. However optimistic we are, this statement makes as little sense as the previous one in which we assume that when a character faces left, then the person is facing the past.

I was happy that my experiment didn't give me any surprises. Again, if we perceive anything, then it's because we have a language to articulate what we see, not because things and events have an inherent meaning and orientation. So we go with that story, namely, that's it's a story we're looking at, not fate or a goal, but a story of our own words. Whether in the mirror or not, the words disclose a state of mind.

The idea of the economy of this started to emerge in my head. How to represent it? After processing my images, toning them in tea, ironing them, cutting them in hand, and gilding them, I was ready to present them accompanied also by a book of Tarot haiku poems. I thought that this form would best express the possibility to not cling to any set conventions, whether temporal, causal, literal or symbolic.

Since the poems engage the images beyond direction – you don't need the actual cards to enjoy this book – they contribute to considering the cards as talismanic objects in the mirror, illusions that you don't hold in your hands, performing the type of magic that is not the result of intuition, symbolic action, and ritual, but rather magic in and out of the arcades of perception.

Spinning carousel

Deserved justice of the fools

The sun loves a winner

Bright constellations

Cast their light on fur and hair

Sin is a free prayer

The eyes in the dark

See the world of core desire

A scepter is lost

No merciful turns

But for the naked command

'Enlightenment now'

Cloak, lamp, no dagger

Being on the spot is wise

But fools don't know that

Winged art and ardor

Theater of wings, hot and pink

Adversary flight

Fearing the dark dream

Is also a path to love

Until hatred strikes

Sun on horizon

Below, hell is bent on force

The moon's crazy gasp

Poems in your face

Deadly ornaments of rite

The world listens fast

Tensioned attention

Non-negotiable power

Blessings in the womb

Devil in details

Crossing legs on a missed path

Books and rites shake hands

Boss of pyramid

Dependent self-reliance

The trick is around

Hereafter circus

Perfect seductions at court

The pun is inside

When Robin Hood hangs

Coins drop on death like hot stars

Mixed and matched robbers

Symmetrical love

Not the domain of the wise

Impermanent rules

Amber for a queen

Enchanted celebration

Race of opinions

Pelted water on

Unholy alliances

Fear at a standstill

The door to the star

A trickster's contemplation

Towering worlds change

A world so perfect

But not enough for the dull

They come without shame

It's always like this

When you have to cut the con

Just diplomacy

Take it easy now

Impressions matter little

The sharp insight rules

A book in your lap

A finger and a scepter

Who knows their syntax?

The face of the law

Not subject to force or flow

Flames won't change a fool

Inevitable

Only she can fix the blast

Give or take, a fool

The straight arrow's heart

The end or start? – false idea

Unconscious envy

Open Sesame

Rolling with the diamond fate

Glimmer in the blade

Fast dexterity

A world of sheer nothingness

Empire of angels

An armored image

Naked self on empty roads

Auspicious outcome

The path less traveled

The monk's kissing of the moon

Lovers meet no end

EPILOGUE

Let me end here with a statistical observation and a point about what motivated me to stop. Anyone who has ever tried writing a haiku will know just what an addictive activity it can be. Obsessive too, because, unless you're a Zen master or some such, possessing perfect clarity, there's the danger of agonizing about the words that fall flat. A writer with no claims to 'higher consciousness' will also be interested in avoiding clichés and formulations that go nowhere.

Because I'm a writer and a Zen inclined person, I have obviously tried to avoid both agony and the flat tone. My solution has been simple: Write everything in one setting, and edit nothing. What is, is. That is to say, what made it on the page in the first try, stayed.

So I wrote all of the above in what amounts to a few hours on a long, rainy afternoon. What made me stop, however, was not so much the inability to continue into the night, but rather the realization that you can *never* stop.

I let the cards decide it for me. I wrote poems until I could see that all the Tarot trumps landed on the table as the pinnacle card at least once. When they all had, I stopped.

Some cards insisted on appearing at the top three times. These cards are the Star and the Wheel of Fortune. I decided that for these particular cards to appear three times at the top was auspicious. We usually wish upon a star and to be lucky in our turnings. When fortune goes around, it's all very good. Thrice the fortune is thrice as good.

Another curious thing was to see that the Hanged Man made it in as many as 13 poems. Is it because he was trying to avoid Death, by embodying its number? Death is 13 in the Tarot.

I could launch into some esoteric discussion of statistical data, frequency of appearing, and avoidance, but I'll be brief and only make a passing comment.

For instance, the Devil was not so comfortable with the haiku. Too much constraint in counting syllables. How about some unruly passion, make a mistake in counting, or indeed, as is more obvious with the Devil, how about some excess somewhere? I had the distinct feeling that the Devil wanted to ask: 'What's in it for me, if I keep showing up in this terse world, one that is at odds with what I entice to?'

Generally speaking, the Devil doesn't like an empty head. I think that his most feared enemy must be a Zen master, who will insist on calling the Devil the result of a projected phenomenon, a distinct idea that arises in the empty mirror, which the mind is. The Devil prefers the excessive illusions that are taken as the real thing, rather than words that deconstruct the world and themselves.

In contrast, the Hanged Man, the one with the least power to act, the one with his mind upside down, wanted the opposite. Contrary to his function to just hang in there, he was all over the place. 'Look,' he seemed to say, 'I can be here 13 times. Isn't it cool?' It wasn't. There were only so many words I could come up with, that would convey the Hanged Man's predicament.

It goes to show. You can never trust shuffling. It's as unpredictable as the Fool, creating repetitive patterns that would make many a conspiracy theorist happy. However, seeing the Fool many times over was not surprising. We expect the Fool to come barging in, stumbling over all sorts of situations and creating them too.

The Popess kept quiet, minding her business and her book. It was clear that she wasn't all that interested in this project. The Hermit on the other hand, had many questions. 'How many syllables, again? What does it all mean?'

'It means what it means,' the Angel of Judgment would say. 'It's all a circus.' 'A controlled circus', the Emperor would say, under the Empress' gaze: 'Wanker,' her eyes said, in resentment of the fact that the Emperor would consort more with the Pope than with her.

The Magician did his best, even though he was not at his most competent. He had his eyes on the World, though, and she lifted him up.

The Sun and the Moon were in conversation, almost resembling the trendy bipolar disorder: 'Now you're high, now you're low. Rejoice. All is well.'

Meanwhile you couldn't argue with Justice. As soon as one tried to do that, boom, the Tower. You can't argue with smashed bricks either.

'Come, come', Temperance would say, 'it's not a disaster.' And so it isn't, for how liberating it is to write this story here, use longer sentences and phrases. None of that incoherent, oracular poetry. Who needs to be frightened by ambiguity?

And yet, and yet. I think the Devil is thinking of something. I wonder what he wants. More words, I'm sure. As I ponder on this, I see that the Hermit is back to flashing his light in my face: 'All these desires. Put them down'.

And so I do, here and now. The world of secret affinities can take care of itself.